FROM ETERNITY PAST THROUGH ETERNITY FUTURE

RUTH LEE

authorHOUSE®

AuthorHouse™
1663 Liberty Drive
Bloomington, IN 47403
www.authorhouse.com
Phone: 833-262-8899

Published by AuthorHouse 09/25/2020

ISBN: 978-1-6655-0109-5 (sc)
ISBN: 978-1-6655-0108-8 (e)

Print information available on the last page.

CONTENTS

PREFACE

The questions of all ages has been, where did I come from, why am I here, and where am I going. Sometime in the past, God created the universe and this earth. Before we were created God said he knew you. So God didn't just happen to create you, you were planned and he knew what his purpose was for you from before you were born, it's our place to find out what that plan is and try to develop it. so that we can be what he wants us to be throughout eternity.

What we are to do here now is to follow God's plan of salvation and be ready for eternity, it is Because of the fall of Satan, and sin entering into the world that has caused man to deviate from the original plan of God. That is why it is needful for us to go through hardships, trials and suffering in this life to prepare us for our future eternal life. because it is through suffering that we learned obedience to God. V 12, 1 Peter 4:12–13 KJV beloved, thank it not strange concerning the fiery darts which h is to try you, as though some strange thing happened unto you: v13 but rejoice, and so much as we are partakers of Christ's suffering; that, when his glory shall be revealed, he may be glad also with exceeding joy.

Where are we going? We're going to a new heaven and earth that God has prepared for us for all eternity, it seems that it is somewhat like this earth, actually it seems that it is this earth. Because it speaks of kings bringing their glory into the Holy City, it's about the kingdoms of this world becoming the kingdoms of our God and his Christ, it speaks of Israel being established in the land forever. So we're not just haphazardly put together, everything has a plan and a purpose and God will see to it that that plan and purposes is carried out in the next life.

INTRODUCTION

As you read this book, you will be experiencing extraordinary visions, supernatural visitations. The knowledge I have gained through the past 55 years from pastors, prophecy teachers, intense study, and of all, what God spoke to me during a recent illness. Which I have woven together for this book, based on what I recently experienced. I was in the hospital for several weeks, followed by rehab centers for several months. Throughout my stays there, many things happened to help me understand God's plan much better. God began speaking to me about creation, "from eternity past through eternity future". I had several encounters with God. He let me experience His presence and talk with Him. I also experienced the black darkness of Satan's kingdom as he made a horrendous attack on my faith. From this. These encounters seem to happen when my heart had stopped and it did, many times before they put the pacemaker in. I want to help those who are interested to understand that it is extremely important that we are aware of the enemy who will do anything to destroy you and your faith. Nothing is easy when you are working for God. We have an enemy to fight all along the way. A good scripture to put into practice during your walk with God is, Nehemiah 4:17 KJV, which says to do your work with one hand while having a sword in the other hand. I pray that you will learn many truths' from this presentation.

Where did I come from, Why am I here, and Where am I going

Sometime in the past, God created the universe and this earth. Before we were created God said he knew you. So God didn't just happen to create you, you were planned and he knew what his purpose was for you from before you were born, it's our place to find out what that plan is and try to develop it. so that we can be what he wants us to be throughout eternity

What we are to do now is to follow God's plan of salvation and be ready for eternity, it is Because of the fall of Satan, and sin entering into the world that has caused man to deviate from the original plan of God. That is why it is needful for us to go through hardships, trials and suffering in this life to prepare us for our future eternal life. because it is through suffering that we learned obedience to God

V 12, 1 Peter 4:12–13 KJV beloved, think it not strange concerning the fiery darts which h is to try you, as though some strange thing happened unto you: v13 but rejoice, and so much as we are partakers of Christ's suffering; that, when his glory shall be revealed, he may be glad also with exceeding joy. Where are we going? We're going to a new heaven and earth that God has prepared for us for all eternity, it seems that it is somewhat like this earth, actually it seems that it is this earth. Because it speaks of kingdoms of this earth become in the kingdoms of our God and his Christ. And kings bringing their glory into the Holy City, it's about the kingdoms of this world becoming the kingdoms of our God and his Christ, it speaks of Israel being established in the land forever. So we're not just haphazardly put together, everything has a plan and a purpose and God will see to it that that plan and purposes is carried out in the next life.

CHAPTER 1

THE BEGINNING OF MY NEW LIFE

Fifteen years I've been away from God living a degenerate lifestyle that I was not a custom to. During that last year of my wandering, I had such a strong desire to return to God I thought I would lose my mind. I believe that is due to the prayers of my parents I realize now that parents do not have to allow Satan to have charge over their children.

During the last year at that time I was so fearful of being eternally lost; I was ready to surrender it has been fifty-seven years since I accepted the Lord as my Savior, it was almost immediately after that commitment I developed an intense interest in the kingdom of God.

My dad was a prophecy teacher. remember as a very young child learning from the big chart he had painted which was frequently displayed across the platform of the church. Especially of interest to me were his drawings of the animals, the horns, the beautiful city, and the new earth

Armed with my daddy's scrapbook, his charts, and my Bible my desire to know more about what I was reading in the Word led me to intensify my study of the Scripture. I was drawn to the supernatural of the Lord.

Being raised in a Christian home has it's advantages. Having good training in my formative years has paid off for me. My family believe in living a holy life, which was inforced with discipline. Being taught the Scriptures those years most likely have played a part in my interest in God and his plan.

My interest in the kingdom of God began fifty-seven years ago after I accepted the Lord as my savior. Using only the Bible and my daddy's scrapbook While studying his notes and even as a very young child I learned a little from the big painted chart he put across the platform. I remember the animals, the horns, the beautiful city, and the new earth. Reading his notes years ago I gained an interest in Scriptures concerning the supernatural, I developed a desire to know more about what I was reading and began to intensify my study.

I had been away from God for fifteen years but for a year or more I had a strong desire to return to God. I thought I would lose my mind I was so fearful of being eternally lost. When I found my way back to God, I was ready to surrender ALL. I developed a strong hatred for Satan for what he had done to me. I vowed to do more for God than I ever had for him. And as of today I have done for more from God than I ever did for him. My favorite place to study God's word was at my dining room table. Suddenly I could only see a thick fog and I was taken aback with it. I said Lord, "I know there's a table, window, and chairs, but I can't see them, but it's OK." Somehow, I knew I had entered in to God's presence even though at that time I was a new Christian and had no knowledge about this glory. I knew it was God

I soon began to gain more knowledge through much research on the kingdom of God and Satan's domain. After fifty-seven years, it is still my main interest as I continue to grow in God.

time I experienced his glory while I was working in a mill. There were people all around. I was praying silently when the Shekinah Glory appeared. I was so overcome with his presence; I knew something was happening, so I went to the rest room lounge. The machinery was so loud no one could hear me. I danced, worshiped, and praised for quite some time. What a night!

Later a group from Brownsville church was in a near by city and I attended the service. That night the Glory cloud appeared - awesome! The next Sunday the cloud was in Pastor Jim's Sunday school class. I can still feel the Glory of God's presence!

CHAPTER 2

VISIBLE ANGELS

I have experienced several contacts with angels, which has had a great impact on my life.

I clean house best when I am unhappy with something my husband Hubert had done and that day I was very upset. I was cleaning and planning to confront him when he got home from work. Suddenly, I was completely surrounded by huge angels looking down on me with an angry frown. I decided I better not do that today.

Angels look just like the ones I'm going to tell you about now. Recently in church, Pastor Greg was speaking on holiness. I said to myself, (not out loud,), "God would you holify me?" And at my left side I heard someone chuckle. I thought, "How could anyone have heard me." I looked around and there was a huge angel standing there with his hand over his mouth. He was actually laughing at me about the made up word I used. holify, so I elbowed him.

I told you earlier how I had developed a communication with God. My relationship with him is many times in the natural. and I would speak to him as though he were human, and maybe be a little lighthearted with him. One example. I was sitting at the window talking to God telling him how much I loved him and then I thought about all the things that he had done for me that week. I said, "God, I don't only love you, I appreciate you!" Immediately a small portion of the venation blinds near the top begin to slowly flow in and out softly about seven times. I looked around to see if it was my air-conditioner; it was not on. I look to see if the wind was blowing outside but, no, it was still. Then I realized that that was a response from God.

Another morning I was enjoying the sunrise and I said, "God everything you do is more beautiful than what man has done." Immediately I heard him say, "Duh-a." God speaks to me many times on my level.

I had a great dad and am using him as an example. I could sit on his lap as a child. He would read to me. I could say things to him in a joking manner; however, in public or when he got serious with me because I was doing something wrong, he was another man to me - a man of honor and integrity, one who demanded respect. Through our relationship I learned how to communicate with God. Yes! God is an awesome God. But he's my Father and friend.

CHAPTER 3

PREPARING FOR ETERNITY FUTURE

I wish I could say that everything goes wonderful when we serve the Lord here on this earth; however, it has never been that way for me. I learn obedience and grow in God when I am going through a trial of some kind.

In March 2018, my heart began to stop and start. I was sitting in my living room when suddenly I lost consciousness with this world and entered into another dimension. I began to go backward into a tunnel with bright blue and red blocks of color. Then I began to come back to this world. That was the beginning of six months of severe illness. Debbie took me to the emergency room.

Shortly after arriving there, a doctor passed by a monitor at the front desk at just the right time and saw my heart stop then start. I heard him say, "Now I know now what is happening. "They rushed me in to surgery to put in a pacemaker. I was aware of what was taking place in the surgical unit. I could hear them talking about my heart going into a block and then they would shock my heart. This occurred three or four times, but I was not disturbed.

In recovery, God put a song in my heart. I began to sing "God leads His Dear Children Along". Debbie was there, and she began to sing along on the chorus with me. I looked up. Jesus was standing on a round white cloud singing back to us. But I could tell by his gestures that he was saying. I told Debbie about it' she was amazed. She asked what he looked like. I said, "He looks the same as he did thirty-eight years ago when he appeared to me during a serious illness.

Being very ill my daughter Laura was concerned about me. She lived in North Carolina then. She called me that afternoon and told me that I had better not die until she could come home.

Later that afternoon Jesus came and stood by my bed. There was a mirror on the wall behind him, but you can see all of the Mirror and all of him. He seemed to be talking to the Spirit.{perhaps an angel} He would look back at me and then back to him. He went away, and I loudly proclaimed, "Come back! I have served you many years and I deserve to know what you're talking about!" So he came back and did the same thing again except this time he looked at me with a big smile. When I smiled back at him, it was like his smile and a mine were one. Very strange experience. I knew that everything would be alright. He went away

Late that evening the spirit (or Angel) that was speaking with Jesus earlier came back and stood at the head of my bed. He began to show me a panoramic view of my life - how I had served the Lord many years, that this is what you have lived for. He said, "You can choose either to go be with the Lord and receive your eternal rewards or you can choose to stay here. It is your choice." I pondered that for awhile then I said, "I choose to stay and declare the word of the Lord." That was a very hard choice to make at that point because there was a strong presence of God there. I also remembered that Laura had asked me to stay here until you could come home. I said to the spirit, "I choose to stay to declare the words of the Lord." I was not sure about that decision, not knowing what the future held. Now I am glad I made that decision. I have had a very fruitful life and much pleasure with my family.

Back in the recovery room, having seen Jesus, my mind was not on my physical condition.

We were across the hall from the nurses' station. They evidently heard us singing. My nurse was a young male. He walked over to the bed and said they are moving me to another area and that he going with me! Of course, he didn't but I'm assuming that he heard us singing. After that God spoke again quoting to me part of the 23rd Psalm. He said, "You have been through the valley of the shadow of death and have feared no evil." I believe that is when I realized it was me being tested. I assume I passed that test

At this point in my life I had surrendered everything to God to the best of my ability to serve Him and others. I had been speaking freely with Him about this for several years. I am thinking he's testing me concerning that

As I was being transported to another area in the hospital, God spoke to me really clear and ask, "Would you be willing to go THROUGH this suffering if it would help someone?" He said he needed to test a certain person. Without knowing what suffering, or what person, I said, "Yes." What he seemed to be saying was that he could heal me, but he needed me to do this for someone.

Now I realize this is more of a spiritual matter then it is a physical matter. We all must be tested; I was aware of that.

Then I was told by the doctor that I needed surgery immediately for colon cancer. I went through the surgery. I never had any pain nor discomfort - not anything that would make me think I had had eight inches of my colon removed - except for weakness. I believe that came from the medication I was allergic to. It was at this time that I had an out-of-this-world experience with God.

CHAPTER 4

CREATION OF THE UNIVERSE

God takes me back to the original creation

At that Point God begin to teach me about creation through the Scriptures. May God grant me the wisdom to explain.

Read--Hebrews11:3 NLT By faith we understand that the entire universe was formed at God's command, that what we now see did not come from anything that can be seen

At some point I was transported far out into the universe. I begin to experience things out of the ordinary such as, I was standing straight, (I said that because I cannot stand straight since the stroke) I was standing beside God and beheld an empty space so huge both sides and in front of me. I cannot explain it, after experiencing all these things that begin to understand that God was showing me the creation of the universe because he knew that later on Satan was going to try to convince me that there was no creation.

God stood beside me but i never look toward him but I could see him without looking toward him, things are far different there than they are here so much clearer so much easier to understand so admirable. He was dressed in a soft gold robe it was almost translucent but not transparent he was a little taller than most men yet he had a shape like a man, I could see that soft golden robe, though I tried I would not be able to touch him. and I never spoke how ever I could understand his thoughts perfectly.

The first thing he said was "in the beginning God" a short pause then he begin to explain God the supreme being. His power, wisdom and abilities the awesomeness of his Glory, the splendor of his presents everything good seemed to be rapt up in one being. He spoke to me about realms, dimensions and spheres then he told me that I could not remember that realm that I was in because, he said if I did I would not be able to function in this sin cursed world.

It did not seem unusual for me to be there. Then he spoke again and said "in the beginning God created the heavens," then he began to show me the creation of the universe first there was the throne of God, bible says there are marrieds of angels around the throne, it stood out in space awesome,

At this time, Stars begin to take their places, milky ways, nebulous, many shapes and forms and colors and world. And the earth took its place prepared for it and for mankind. the stars zooming through the atmosphere, different types of planets and moons and black holes begin to take there place in the universe as God spoke to them and told them where to go,

He knew that I was questioning him in my mind of where they came from and then he said, my hands hath made them. I noticed the brilliance of the lights that were coming in from behind me but I never turned to look I could see them without turning, things are not the same there as they are here we're not inhibited or hindered from experiencing the supernatural. and he said in earthly terms, that is my workshop where i designed the universe and all that is in it,

Every star has a name everything I do has a purpose and a plan, again I heard him say, "in the beginning God created the heavens and the earth." At that point he begin to show me the creation of the earth placing everything where it belonged, Seems the garden of Eden is a very special place everything in it is enough to sustain man forever, every tree and plant is there to meet the needs of man.

Also the animals all of his creation is so purposeful. I wish I had the words to explain the awesomeness of this creation but there is no way, no words. Connecting scriptures helps us to see more clearly. Scriptures tells us about his heavenly beings, the heavenly hosts, angels, 33:14-15, Colossians 1:16-20 KJV For by him were all things created, that are in heaven, and that are in earth, visible and invisible, whether they be thrones, or dominions, or principalities, or powers: all things were created by him, and for him: What is this creation like? to me it's a beautiful green earth decorated with all kind of beautiful flowers fruit and nut trees blossoming trees, grass, all kind of animals, Fish birds, butterflies, skunks and snakes ETC. Most Bible scholars think, that everything man has ever needed to live a full happy life, was created. The bible says that every seed bearing tree was good for food. I'm wonder just how many other things we have not yet discovered in the world about his provisions.

1 Corinthian 2:9 KJV But as it is written, Eye hath not seen, nor ear heard, neither have entered into the heart of man, the things which God hath prepared for them that love him. But God has revealed them on to us by his spirit.

The creation of man

1 Corinthians 13: 12 KJV For now we see through a glass, darkly, but then face-to-face. Now I know in part; but then shall I know, even as also I am known. Isaiah 45:18 KJV For thus saith the LORD that created the heavens; God himself that formed the earth and made it; he hath established it, he created it not in vain, he formed it to be inhabited: I am the LORD; and there is none else.

Colossians 1:16-20 KJV For by him were all things created, that are in heaven, and that are in earth, visible and invisible, whether they be thrones, or dominions, or principalities, or powers: all things were created by him, and for him:

God says, that he created man to have fellowship with him communicate with him someone that would worshiping and acknowledge him as God. As humans we learn more about what we see, so looking at man, you can see more what God is like. not the fallen nature, but the undefiled five senses, emotion, character and all of his nature. Just because God is spirit does not mean he does not have these things.

CHAPTER 5

WHAT ARE ANGELS

Heaven is a place of extraordinary activities, things are happening with the Seraphim's which have six wings with two they cover there faces with two they cover there lower bodies, and with two they do fly, they call back and forth as they circle the throne saying Holy Holy Holy unto the Lord. Isaiah 6:3, worshipers.

Cherubim's are said to be guardians of the throne and they guard the garden of Eden, and the way of the tree of life. Geneses. Cherubim's seem to be Gods main transportation also, Ezekiel saw a storm rolling in a very frightening experience, it turned out to be the throne being borne by cherubim's having a sea of glass in front of it, Ez. 28:14 KJV tells us Lucifer was a cherubim before the fall.

Gabriel is thought to be a messenger of God to the Gentile nations, Michael seems to be for Israel, arch-angels, guardian angels, ministering spirits, some are sent to individuals bearing either messages or answers to prayer. Psalms 91:11 KJV. One writer said, there seems to be angels watching over and taking care of everything for the Lord and us. Some are called ministering spirits. Its not all beings in heaven are classified as angels there seems to be other type beings. Even though we may tend to classify them all his angels.

Fall of Satan

The first reference to the morning star as an individual is in Isaiah 14:12 NIV: "How you have fallen from heaven, morning star, son of the dawn! You have been cast down to the earth, you who once laid low the nations!" (NIV). The KJV and NKJV both translate "morning star" as "Lucifer, son of the morning." It is clear from the rest of the passage that Isaiah is referring to Satan's fall from heaven, Satan was created a cherubim the bible said, he was the cherub that covered Job 38:7 KJV: When the morning stars sang together, and all the sons of God shouted for joy? angels are innumerable.

God originally created everything to be good However Satan and man polluted the whole world and our atmosphere. That is why Jesus came to earth, to restore us and the earth. His new heaven and new earth is possibly going to be like He originally created it, in order for it to be that way, there has to be a restoration and cleansing from all the evil Satan and man has caused. This must be done by fire, not water like in the days of Noah. Water washes, fire destroys. He has already preformed a restoration on the church. 2 Corinthian 5:17 NIV Therefore, if any man is in Christ, he is a new creature old things have passed away,behold all things have become new. the person did not pass away only the evil that was in him. Scriptures says that about the earth, Using the same Greek word. Old things will pass away an all things become new, not to be remembered no more, the same as our sins.

Geneses, God told Adam to till the garden. He put him to work soon after creation. Work is a great part of Gods kingdom when Satan deceive man work become labor. Hebrews 2:11 KJV explains how He is no longer ashamed to call us brothers and sisters. Therefore our work is to God, and has undying value, whether it be provinces or nations working alongside God. As one writer puts it, "we are co-creators with him." That would be on a lower level. Jesus said we are joint heirs with Him and will reign with Him. There is a outstanding purpose for what we do here on earth. The book of Hebrews explains how not only we but the earth is in need of a restoration. Jesus is the one supremely in charge of the creation and only by working in him are we restored to fellowship with God. This alone makes us capable to take our place again as vice-regents of God on earth. Humanity's created destine is being achieved in Christ, in whom we find the pattern. Evil plays a strong hand at present and heaven and earth is in need of radical restoration. Hebrews is trying to show, because it is now subject to evil, therefore is subject to radical restoration.

Malachi 4:1 KJV

Sickness from medication

After God stopped talking and showing me things, I was Back in intensive care

Next, the medication I was allergic to Had made me weak so that i could not eat or drink for many days, my team of doctors came in that did the pacemaker surgery, I knew something needed to be done or i wasn't going to make it so I became very serious with the doctor, that I was getting worse they had promised i would be all better after the pacemaker surgery. But meantime just after the Dr. left the room Laura, Debbie and my granddaughters Heather were in the room and I told them, get that bottle of oil out of the drawer and anoint me and pray THE prayer of faith this was like a command from heaven, After anointing me with oil we started praying and then Debbie stop and said I don't know how to pray! Then she thought about what the bible says, when you don't know what to pray let the spirit pray through you because he knows what to pray So we all stopped and begin to pray in the spirit all four of us. It was at that point that i began to get thirsty and hungry that was so different from what it had been I had not been able to eat or drink very much, for over two weeks just one or two bites at a time. And it was from that point I started to improve from the effects of the medication. (for those of you who are not Pentecost praying in the spirit is when you pray in a language that you have not learned. Tongues of men and of Angels.

A Covenant with God

Before I explain what happens next, I want to tell you about a commitment I made with God in about 1963, I told him if you will help me I will do everything I can for you throughout all my life because I don't want to be an ordinary Christian and I don't want to receive an ordinary reward. I want the most extraordinary place in heaven that I can possibly have. have thoroughly enjoyed my walk with the Lord, I still want to do everything I can as long as I can for God. I Believe I will receive my reward but I would do it for Him at this point in my walk with God, if there was no rewards. I have kept my agreement through the years, no matter how Hard the suffering, pain or distress.

CHAPTER 6

SATANIC ATTACK

Looking back at the question God ask me about suffered so someone could be tried, seems that this next test I'm going through is the purpose of all my suffering. I was incoherent a lot of the time that is when one of them would speak. It's like each time the enemy would come and put negative thoughts in my mind before long God would come and teach me truth and positive thing, This was the first attack from satan. I was no longer on the earth, I wonder if this is one of the times my heart had stopped? I could see myself as though I was suspended somewhere in space, there was a bank of white clouds behind me and I was not standing straight, I was bent over, I could see a Spirit, it said, you Actually on the outskirts of my dwelling place. I believe he was trying to imitate God, taking me into the universe. I could see him everything was black dark but he resembled a orange ball with the orange glow around it. Actually he is a poor imitator.

Second horrendous attac

As I pondered this in counter, I'm thinking that God let me stand with him and see the universe being created so I could make a choice we have to make choices all through our lives. I thank God he counted me worthy to go through this experience. I'm thinking that God let me stand with him and see the universe being created so I would have a choice of whom i would believe. As I was waking up from the colon surgery, I had an out of the ordinary attack from Satan. he spoke out of the blackness of darkness saying, "you say you believe in God and heaven, how do you know it's true, look up, what do you see" There is no universe, there is no God, it's just me. I could not see a thing it was pitch black no stars or anything. I thought, even if I cant see it I still believe it is there. it seems I am now outside, but it was all black darkness. He said, many people believe many things about heaven and God but it does not make it true, it's just a figment of your imagination.

My mind was clouded with his doubts, He went on in that darkness for a long time until I was very weary, and he began to tell me "you have lost the reward you asked God for years ago, because you told God you did not want to suffer." Of course I don't remember doing that. he told me that i did that while I was asleep he continued bombarding my mind with negative thoughts for days, he was very convincing. I am really tired of this fierce battle, I began to strongly rebuke him, then I declared, I'm going with Jesus all the way. I choose to believe in heaven and in Jesus even if I cant see it now.

And I spoke to God saying, God I do not believe I did that, I cannot believe that I would give up anything in heaven, to avoid a little suffering, I never did it before I don't believe I've done it now. For many weeks Satan attacked my mind telling me I did give it up you just cant remember, he was extremely convincing. he kept Saying, I would not have anything except Heaven. Sometimes it would be days between these encounters with God and with my enemy then God would challenge me to see the truth. Reminding me of miracles he had done for me.

20

Miracle

This is one of them, God preformed many miracles for me, one was shortly after Debbie and Wes were married, they both took a job at a 711 store, it was a nighttime job. i always thought that was not safe. One night after i had retired for the night about 11:00 God spoke to me that one of my family was in danger, I thought it was Debbie so I got up dressed and drove to the store, but she assured me that everything was alright, so i got in my car and headed home even more disturbed, so i held my hand out toward the store and said, regardless of Debbie, or Wesley regardless of the Devil or any thing else no body will enter that store to do harm and they will not work there anymore I went home but the next morning Debbie called and said mama the store where Wesley works was robbed last night an one man was killed another wounded. The man killed was standing where Wesley would have been. she wonder why i didn't pray for both stores, I did pray for Wesley's safety but not the store. i was thinking God was warning me about her store so I am thinking i needs to be more thoughtful about how i prays. We are here on this earth to be armed and available when he needs. knowing now that this is what God was speaking of when he asked me would I go through this, I do know for sure now that it was me that he was testing and you will understand it better as you go along in the book why I had experiences with both God and the devil. I had surrendered everything to God to the best of my ability, to serve Him and others. I have been speaking freely with Him about this for several years. I am thinking he's testing me concerning that.

CHAPTER 7

WHAT TS GOD ACTUALLY LIKE

Once In my private place of warship I asked, God, what are you really like? he replied, I am more natural than you think, and I am more spiritual than you think. So I understood from that encounter that I needed to upgrade my knowledge of him. I found man has more of the nature of God than I thought, but He also was more of a spiritual being then I realized. So i began an intensive study about God and his creation. So we know his spiritual nature is to be all powerful, all-knowing and everywhere present. But do we really understand what that means, we understand his natural side better. Man being made in the image of God looking at men's emotions and characteristics helps us to know his nature better, So man has Gods nature, but at mans best, he seem to give to much control to self and the enemy.

Seem like days I was not fully conscious of what was going on, then I heard Laura, singing "Soon and very soon we are going to see the king." at this point I don't think she had much hope of me recovering, seems that was what everyone was thinking. However, God took care of everything concerning the surgery. I didn't seem to be affected except for the weakness, and I have been improving since. No, I'm still not completely well, but I am on my way.

How can we know God

Before this sickness I had ask God a Question,

In my private place of warship I asked, God, what are you really like? he replied, I am more natural than you think, and I am more spiritual than you think. So I understood from that encounter that I needed to upgrade my knowledge of him. I found man has more of the nature of God than I thought, but He also was more of a spiritual being then I realized. So i began an intensive study about God and his creation. So we know his spiritual nature is to be all powerful, all-knowing and everywhere present. But do we really understand what that means, we understand his natural side better. Man being made in the image of God looking at men's emotions and characteristics helps us to know his nature better, So man has Gods nature, but at mans best because of our fallen nature, he seems to give to much control to self and the enemy.

CHAPTER 8

THE CREATION OF HEAVEN AND THE EARTH

1 Cor.2:9 KJV as it is written: "What no eye has seen, what no ear has heard, and what no human mind has conceived"— the things God has prepared for those who love him. But God has revealed them on to us by his spirit.1 Corinthians 13: 12 KJV For now we see through a glass, darkly, but then face-to-face. Now I know in part; but then shall I know, even as also I am known. What is this creation like? to me it's a beautiful green earth decorated with all kind of beautiful flowers fruit and nut trees blossoming trees, grass, all kind of animals, Fish birds, butterflies, skunks and snakes ETC.

Most Bible scholars think, that everything man has ever needed to live full happy life, was created. The bible says that every seed bearing tree was good for food. I'm wonder just how many other things we have not yet discovered in the word about his provisions. Then he made man, IN HIS IMAGE,I asked God many years ago why did he create such a great universe and earth. speak back to my heart that it was for his son and his sons Bride Isa. 45:18 KJV For thus saith the LORD that created the heavens; God himself that formed the earth and made it; he hath established it, he created it not in vain, he formed it to be inhabited: I am the LORD; and there is none else. Colossians 1:16-20 King James Version (KJV)For by him were all things created, that are in heaven, and that are in earth, visible and invisible, whether they be thrones, or dominions, or principalities, or powers: all things were created by him, and for him

Familiar Spirits, imitators

Back in the hospital room Now, Things in the hospital room are i am still sleeping most of the time, I awoke and my dad who has been dead for about 44 years appeared at the head of my bed dressed as he did in the 30s and 40s working in the field. He didn't say anything he just walked around. Then I saw my sister and two brothers they were much younger than they were when they went to be with the Lord they were standing side by side, still and not talking. They were just on the other side of the wooden rail fence which we had around our property in those days, and behind them was a huge field but there was not a blade of grass not a tree it was totally empty everything was dead, my dad was also behind the fence up toward my head, the girls heard me say, how did you get here? they ask,who do you see? I said Papa, can't you see him. Most every one thought for sure at that point I was not going to make it. But I knew better. That lasted for quite a while and then they were gone. I begin to try to tell people about it but the Lord did not seem to approve of me telling it, so I didn't mention it to but just two or three people then later Satan said, see the dead grass see the old fence that represents that you have nothing laid up in heaven it's all gone is dead. But God was with me I had explicit confidence in God that He would not allowed Satan to defeat me. I didn't have a dread or fear my heart was fixed,

I begin to realize something did not seem right and ponder what was going on, I begin to realize it was Satan sending familiar spirits. You might ask, What is a familiar spirit? It's evil spirit, one of the things they do is follow you around Learning your Ways and your mannerisms so they can imitate. I realized that was the way people dressed in the 1930s and 40s so it was those spirits from that time which had observing my family they had come in the form of my family. that was not a visitation from my family for God, I believe Satan did that to make my family think I was not going to live so they would not try to believe for my healing, I am delighted to say, the spirits didn't do a good job at all, my sister never wore red and she had a red blouse on, I suppose they didn't know all that much about them we were always a lively family.

anyone who had done anything for me he would give them whopping reward I thought extraordinaire sound better so I put extraordinary but God spoke immediately and said I did not say extraordinary I said whopping. so I changed it back to whopping, we have to be careful not to think that we know more than God.

Then God talk to me about Job, saying, most people think that was a unique experience, but it seems to be for an example to everyone because we all must be tried.

A challenge from the word.

Hebrews 12:1 NIV says since we are surrounded by such a great cloud of witnesses., Let us throw off everything that hinders and the sin that does so easily in tangles us.

22 But you have come to Mount Zion and to the city of the living God, the heavenly Jerusalem, and to innumerable angels in festal gathering, 23 and to the assembly of the firstborn who are enrolled in heaven, and to God, the judge of all, and to the spirits of the righteous made perfect, 24 and to Jesus, the mediator of a new covenant, and to the sprinkled blood that speaks a better word than the blood of Abel.

Seems there are things taken place it we're not aware of. Because of this, we need to be more aware of how we live in this present life.

Through the years God has sent his ministers with his words to declare what will happen in the last days and in the future. also showing things that are taking place in heaven now. God has spent many thousands of years trying to develop a people that would follow, love him and worship him so that he could give them the things that he had prepared.

Different types of Angels

1. Seraphim's, Worshipers Isaiah 6:1 KJV
2. Cherubim's, cover Gods throne Gen.3:24 KJV Ezekiel 1:6 KJV
3. Archangels, Michael Gabriel special messengers Daniel 10:13 Michael Has spiritual authority. (He is the Chief prince} he seems to stand for Israel, Gabriel came to Mary, and Hezekiah
4. Principalities, rulers heads of some angel

Eph 1:21 Gods Angels KJV,

5. Powers, Warrior
6. 11, Ezk. 1:21-28 KJV Thrones, carry Gods throne
7. 10, Dominions Eph, 1:21 KJV Gods Angels
8. Ministering spirits, Heb.1:14 KJV
   Ministering to heirs of salvation.
9. Guardian angels
   There seems to be an angel for every purpose under heaven.

Eph. 6:12 KJV fallen Angels

Principalities (Arche, Chief Ruler of the unseen world system

First in Rank or First in existence) Doles out unholy orders to other evil spirits, He is Anti-Christ Spirit,

Powers. This one tries to overpower you physically mentally in any other way.

Powers to Blind people to the truth, and cause many other devastating things because of the blindness to the things of God.

Spiritual Wickedness, evil in both spiritual and physical realm. Our hope is in Christ Jesus who said,

Romans 8:38 KJV For I am persuaded that neither death nor life, nor angels nor principalities nor powers, nor things present nor things to come,

Another challenge

Don't give up. Give out, and don't Give

For those of you who are suffering from Spiritual or emotional struggles, Financial, any other

A. DONT GIVE UP

During these time of trouble be careful not to surrender to Satan's suggestion such as,

There no need to try, your family will never change. Or your not expected to be hurt by your companion so long you just need to get our of that marriage. Another one There on hope, look how long this sickness, Or other problems have been going on.

If you have been Crushed by; Feebleness, sin, troubles *Isaiah 43:24 KJV*

A bruised reed Shall he not break –

He will not carry on the work of destruction, and entirely crush or break it. And the idea is, that he will not make those already broken down with a sense of sin and with calamity, more wretched He will have an affectionate regard for the broken-hearted, the humble, the penitent, and the afflicted.

Isaiah 61:1 KJV, where it is said of the Messiah, ‹He hath sent me to bind up the broken-hearted; 'and to the declaration in Isaiah 50:4, said, ‹that I should know how to speak a word in season to him that is weary.' God said, he will carry you through Take it to Jesus, and don't forget to leave it the B, Don't give out.

Isaiah 43:24 KJV a smoking flax shall he not quench, (wick on a lamp) till he send forth judgment unto victory. –

Satan will say, you have toiled so long, your give our, Its not worth the struggle, your tired, take a break, think about how long you have been doing this, no need to keep preying

C, Don't give in

Satan will try to say, why struggle with sin, if you will do this one more time that will satisfy you. It wont hurt anything, God forgives. then you can get back on the straight and narrow. Remember Sampson he laid his head in the Delilahs lap just one time too many.

So don't ever give up, don't ever give out, and don't ever give in.

CHAPTER 9

THE RAPTURE

The next event on this earths agenda seems to be the rapture of the church, first Thessalonians 4; 15- 17 KJV in a moment, in the twinkling of an eye, at the last trump: the Trumpet shall sound, and the dead in Christ shall rise. Some point during this time a marvelous thing will happened we're all going to the marriage supper of the lamb. Can you imagine state of the art decorations, food, fellowship it's the beginning of his promise of our joy forever more, it tops all banquets Like when we take Jesus told his disciples, at the last supper or communion, that he would not drink of that cup anymore, until he drank it new in the kingdom, take communion with us to seal our relationship with him, God uses things we know about to explain his plan. a good example is a wedding. It starts like this, the bridegroom comes to the brides house he asked her father for his daughter hand in marriage. Brings a dowry, before he leaves they take communion to seal their relationship after that if a couple separate, there has to be a divorce. Then the groom goes to prepare a home for them, the father tells the son when to go get his bride. Likewise, Jesus said, I go to prepare a place for you, the Father will tell Jesus when everything is ready, and to come for us (our communion has a much deeper meaning than what we understand) Jesus do this until I come. Another example is when father Abraham sent his servant to get a bride for son Isaiah. Father God sent his Holy Spirit to get his Son Jesus a bride. "we will understand it better by an by".

Battle of Armageddon

The world, it appears, is spinning faster and faster, heading toward the end of the age and the sure coming rule of Christ.

Revelations 16:14 ESV For they are demonic spirits, performing signs, who go abroad to the kings of the whole world, to assemble them for battle on the great day of God the Almighty. Just before Christ retunes to this earth, the battle of Armageddon is raging, then hundred lb. hailstones falls Isaiah 13:9 Sometime after that, Suddenly, Christ will splits the eastern sky's with his saints sitting on a white horse then he sets his feet on the mount of olives and the mountains splits in half Mat.24:27 as far as the lightening shines from the east to the west, so shall the coming of the son of man be. After he takes care of that evil army that are trying to destroy Gods people, [You don't want to mess with Gods family]

Then He begins to set up his kingdom here on earth, and he will rule and we will reign with him for 1000 years So, when he returns we don't go to heaven at that time not for a thousand years. You cant have peace as long as the devil is around, so God goes ahead and takes care of that in verse 20 Then I saw an angel descending from heaven, holding in his hand the key to the abyss and a huge chain. ² He seized the dragon—the ancient serpent, who is the devil and Satan—and tied him up for a thousand years. ³ The angel then threw him into the abyss and locked and sealed it so that he could not deceive the nations until the one thousand years were finished. This 1000 year reign of Christ is peace, prosperity, long life, How awesome this world will be. Revelation 20:7-9 ESV "And when the thousand years are ended Satan will be released from his prison and will come out to deceive the nations that are at the four corners of the earth, Gog and Magog, to gather them for battle; their number is like the sand of the sea. And they marched up over the broad plain of the earth and surrounded the camp of the saints and the beloved city, but fire came down from heaven and consumed them. And the devil who deceived them was thrown into the lake of fire and sulfur, where the beast and the false prophet are too, and they will be tormented there day and night forever and ever.

CHAPTER 10

GREAT WHITE THRONE JUDGEMENT

As things are winding down we have one more judgment and that is for the wicked the (great white throne judgment.)Do everything you know to do to avoid this judgement. [11] Then I saw a large white throne and the one who was seated on it; the earth and the heaven fled from his presence, and no place was found for them. [12] And I saw the dead, the great and the small, standing before the throne. Then books were opened, and another book was opened—the book of life. So the dead were judged by what was written in the books, according to their deeds. [13] The sea gave up the dead that were in it, and Death and Hades gave up the dead that were in them, and each one was judged according to his deeds. [14] Then Death and Hades were thrown into the lake of fire. This is the second death—the lake of fire. [15] If anyone's name was not found written in the book of life, that person was thrown into the lake of fire. Gets even more awesome, a day we all longed for. This world, all evil and lies and hypocrisy, Will be totally consumed with fire. The atmosphere where Satan set up his kingdom. Totally rolled back like a scroll the elements will melt with fervent heat. No more room for him in the air. It is the evil works of man, the enemy and his kingdom that will be burned up, the area where Satan the has set up his copycat throne.

And ruled over the principalities of the air. Sounds like he gets rid of everything that is not holy and that is not his plan. And is replacing it with brand-new things Beyond our comprehension, it is for our pleasure.

CHAPTER 11

THE NEW JERUSALEM

God is now ready to show us our Capitol city

Rev. 21:2 NIV John says, "I saw the Holy City, the new Jerusalem, coming down out of heaven from God" what an experience! A foursquare golds city studied with all kinds of gyms at the foundation. its brilliance is incomprehensible. Inside the city he describes Gods throne with a sea of glass before it.

Nations will walk in the light of that city and kings will bring there riches there

I heard it describes it like this.

The City at the center of the future Heaven is called the New Jerusalem. Everyone knows what a city is—a place with buildings, streets, and residences occupied by people and subject to a common government. Cities have inhabitants, visitors, bustling activity, cultural events, and gatherings involving music, the arts, education, religion, entertainment, and athletics. If the capital city of the New Earth doesn't have these defining characteristics of a city, it would seem misleading for Scripture to repeatedly call it a city.

Over the years, people have told me they can't get excited about the New Jerusalem because they don't like cities. But this city will be different—it will have all the advantages we associate with earthly cities but none of the disadvantages. The city will be filled with natural wonders, magnificent architecture, thriving culture—but it will have no crime, pollution, sirens, traffic fatalities, garbage, or homelessness. It will truly be Heaven on Earth. Good news translation. Rev. 21:24 KJV) The gates of that city has a name written thereon. These names are the names of the Twelve Tribes of the Sons of Israel (Rev. 21:12 KJV). This means that New Jerusalem is the future permanent home of the redeemed of the nation of Israel. Since the twelve gates have the names of the twelve tribes of the sons of Israel written on them, and since there are twelve foundation stones with the names of the twelve apostles on them, New Jerusalem is to be the home of both the redeemed of Israel and of the Church. There is a correlation, I believe, between the 24 names and the fact that in heaven there are 24 elders (Rev. 4:4, 10; 5:8; 11:16; 19:4 KJV). I believe these 24 elders include twelve elders of Israel and twelve elders of the Church. They are presently in heaven, but they will inhabit New Jerusalem throughout eternity. It is impossible to state with certainty the identities of any of these elders. It is altogether possible that the twelve elders representing the Church are the twelve apostles, Paul being Christ's likely replacement for Judas.

What is the significance of the fact that each gate is a pearl? John Phillips writes, "How appropriate! All other precious gems are metals or stones, but a pearl is a gem formed within the oyster— the only one formed by living flesh. The humble oyster receives an irritation or a wound, and around the offending article that has penetrated and hurt it, the oyster builds a pearl. The pearl, we might say, is the answer of the oyster to that which injured it. The glory land is God's answer, in Christ, to wicked men who crucified heaven's beloved and put Him to open shame. How like God it is to make the gates of the new Jerusalem of pearl. The saints as they come and go will be forever reminded, as they pass the gates of glory, that access to God's home is only because of Calvary. Think of the size of those gates! Think of the supernatural pearls from which they are made! What gigantic suffering is symbolized by those gates of pearl! Throughout the endless ages we shall be reminded by those pearly gates of the immensity of the sufferings of Christ. Those pearls, hung eternally at the access routes to glory, will remind us forever of One who hung upon a tree and whose answer to those who injured Him was to invite them to share His home. as quoted in *The MacArthur New Testament Commentary*, Revelation 12-21 KJV

The New Heaven and New Earth

Paul, John and Isaiah begins to describe what happens next. Israel possessing their land. Jesus has taken care of this worlds system and replacing it with his. Look at what he says.

Paul says in 1 Corinthians 15: 24 KJV Then comes the end, when he shall put Down all rules and all authority and power.

Revelations 11:15 NIV John said. seventh angel sounded his trumpet, and there were loud voices in heaven, which said: "The kingdom of the world has become the kingdom of our Lord and of his Messiah, and he will reign for ever and ever." and ev Isaiah 60:21says it this way,

Thy people also shall be all righteous: they shall inherit the land for ever, the branch of my planting, the work of my hands, that I may be glorified.

Isaiah 9:7 KJV the increase Of his government and Peace there shall be no and, upon the throne of David, and upon his kingdom, to order it, and to establish it with judgment and with justice from henceforth even for ever the Lord of hosts Will perform it. [4] The Lord said to Abram after Lot had parted from him, "Look around from where you are, [15] All the land that you see I will give to you and your offspring forever...so that the Lord will bring about for Abraham what he has promised him.

CHAPTER 12

O GLORIOUS DAY

This is the day that all Christians have been longing for, the sufferings that is going on now will be no more no more pain, death no more sorrow, crying, and heartaches that will all be gone forever. John saw, A New heaven and new earth, why a new one will it be like this earth? Because this whole earth has been polluted by Satan, its pollution has to go, And so does he. We see from the scriptures that it's all going to be burned up rolled back like a scroll everything there has to be gone and replaced with all things new. Eph. 3:21 KJV

21 Do you ever wonder what we will be doing? will we have to work? Instead of labor I believe it would be more like an opportunity to create something. Many people believe that Whatever your heart desires. That is possible, seeing he knows our every thought he would know what we enjoy doing. made us and he will meet your every desire. We will live in our new home happy ever after. When he said I make all things new, could means that it will be made new as we were made new in Christ. The word news is the same Greek word used when he said he would make all things new on this New earth – koinos. At least we know it well be wonderful the absence of evil and that will be awesome. Seems that we are being prepared now on this earth, for what we will be doing in heaven that is if you using the gifts and talents, that God has given you here. As I said earlier

it's more like opportunities that will be a pleasure then. Where there is a kingdom there is lots of work and activities. God does nothing without a purpose so I'm convinced that his purpose is to make us into the person that we are supposed to be now. The best description of our resurrected bodies is, Jesus, He said I am the first fruits of all resurrection. Which is to say, look at his resurrected body, he ate, cooked, you could touch him, walked around, Talked. It appears that we are going to be very active in our new life and new environment.

God created the heavens and the earth, then he told Adam keep the garden, I wonder if this new earth will be more like restoration than a new one. Don't sound like we will just be floating around on some cloud idle all day. Sounds more like we will be enjoying our duties, praising and worshiping God forever. There will be according to the bible, an earth, nations, kingdoms, kings lets see what Jesus said. Eyes have not seen, nor ears heard neither has it interred into the hearts of man what God has prepared for those who love Him. But it has been revealed to those who love Him.

Revelations 11:15 KJV –Isaiah 9:7 KJV Romans 8: 18 KJV

I challenge for you today is, if you don't know Jesus I would like to help you get to know him, then find you a wonderful church that teaches the entire word of God, and that will lead you into a deeper walk with God.

If you want to be apart of this kingdom without end, then you have an open invitation to come to Jesus and start your journey to that holy city New Jerusalem. E-mail me at mrbl22@aol.com and I will be happy to introduce you to our wonderful Lord. And further instruct you on how to live.

RECOGNITIONS

My greatest thanks is to Jerry Byler. Had it not been for him there would be no book. God has allowed him to catch the vision when I told him what God had revealed to me. You have given so much to this book and to the video.

I want to say thank to Linda Mise for her help. She has been so much help in many ways, Thanks to Sandra Newsome for editing this manuscript, doing the finishing touches on it. She stepped in at a time of my need and put it all together. Great job Sandra. My daughter Debbie Blankenship has been a great encouragement as well as daughter Laura Ribelin, to Hope Thornton for helping me keep this computer up and going.

May God's richest blessings be all of you. now through eternity